The Back Door

THE BACK DOOR

poems by

Annie Callan

 Trask House Books
Portland, Oregon

Acknowledgements

Some of the poems herein previously appeared in the following
publications:

> The Antioch Review: Echo; Zen, and More
> The Malahat Review: Lament for the Wanderer
> The Next Parish Over: Irish-American Writing: Home
> Orphic Lute: Irish Aubade
> Poem: Having Spoken Only Once
> Poetry Wales: Heart Attack, Elegance
> Into the 21st Century: Quad City Arts Immigrant Writing: Dawn;
>   The Man at Immigration; Waitress at the Irish Pub
> Rain City Review: Waitress at the Irish Pub
> The Swansea Review: Copper; Why I Cannot Marry the Art Critic

Grateful acknowledgement is due to Oregon Literary Arts for the
1994 William Stafford Poetry Fellowship, which allowed me to finish
this book.

Library of Congress Cataloging-in-Publication Data

Callan, Annie.
    The back door / Annie Callan.
        p.   cm.
    ISBN 0-932264-10-7
    I. Title.
    PS3553.A4219B33   1955
    811'.54--dc20

                                                    95-25709
                                                    CIP

Contents

For Mum and Dad,

thanks for keeping the door open,
or at least leaving the key where I could find it!

Oisín Travelling

has made a gypsy
                    of our tribe

so that now
              our hearts can never

be stilled.
               We can never choose to clot

our own blood.
                  He should have stayed put.

What earthly good
                    can come

from holding a thing twice?
                              But that is

his legacy to us:
                    May you always

be drifting.
              Let you find

some remnant
                 hood of memory

that you may
              bind me to.

Dawn

The clock sirens me from sleep quickly.
Somewhere a crescent moon is startling a sky.
It would be, if not bliss, then easy
to call up that soft deep place again
where responsibility has its own systems,
time its own device, where sense is
what you make it, or do not.

It is November. There is frost, first
winter bite. I am a slow willow rising. I would
stoke last night's embers, if I had a stove, stir
some heat, some light into this small room. If
I had a knife, I'd carve a thick crust off the soda loaf,
skewer, burn it in the rising heat, maybe stew more tea.
But that's another life.

I live alone, almost thirty three, and grateful
for luxuries of cold, hard-thinking space, of walls
that can contain me, and windows that allow a flint
of light. I dreamed of a shut door for three decades;
I have it now. We dig our own graves slowly.

There is another country. It smells of coal
and rubber burning, chimneys and choked sewers,
a river at low tide. It is a foul place sometimes,
and not so peopled now, but there is a certain
blueblack light that saves the early riser.
Factory stacks are burning across town,
hugging huddled laborers. And I am ten
and crying, under the stairs, hearing above
the clock's steady ticking on the mantel
that familiar voice repeat, "It won't always
be dark at six."

Home

My father lies
at the back
of the house,
huge bed hoarding
his room, arm outstretched
as if to embrace
a stranger
or a friend, the door
he likes always open

and my mother sleeps
in front, surrounded
by photographs, jewelry,
lavender potpourri beneath
a peach pillowcase: two
loved ones cornering

the house
where I learned
to listen

and I, in between,
sleepless
at 3 a.m., stars
dot the sky
and all seems
calm.

Biology

Always, after the August rains,
after the last bell unfettered us
from books and uniforms,
we raced across fields,
waded through sawsedge and bogrush
down to the turlough's edge
to cast gilly nets deep
into our secret fen.

Hours we stood,
knee-deep in callows,
air heavy with damsel
and dragonflies,
waiting for fish to cut
through clover and watermint.
Mostly, they stayed away
but, wellies mulching
back up the lane,
we filled our jars anyway
with the odd spotted ladybird
or fistfuls of *fraughan*
from stray branches.
We never came home empty-handed
until that autumn day,
ugly with heat,
we found a pool of tadpoles,
glorious sheaves, and ladled them
fast into glass, laughing
at our slime-brightened faces.
A rustle in the reeds
made us look up
and there he stood,
lacquered and musked,

grinning at you.
Your eyes turned strange,
I watched you unleash your plait,
wipe muck from your cheeks
and toss your jar into the sedge.
I watched the tadpoles squirm away
while he took your hand.

Slouching home behind you,
I wanted to whistle
or crawl through the marsh,
but all I could do was spit.

1930 in Sepia

for Da

You're maybe ten and smiling in your Sunday getup,
mischief giggling out of each big almond eye.
You rest your hip against the gleaming bumper
of your uncle's spiffy car as if you owned it.
Your skinny knees are scuffed with mud or bruises.
I want to stick a shilling behind your ear,
send you spinning to the shops for ice cream.
I want to ask you if you'll play handball
in the alley after Mass lets out. Or tell you
you'll be famous one day. Or whisper gently
father, oh dear sad father, never let that soft
fancy leak out of your brimming face.

Copper

was the color of my mother's marriage ring
when it washed up two years later on the strand,
peagreen flecks fighting through filigree:
the band she'd left behind that bleak day she swam too far
out in her husband's land. A bride, caught
between jellyfish and him.

He could not save her.

He never learned to swim. She found her own way in,
red-streaked, stinging, but not before she gave up
the loose spun gold to seaweed.

By the time it appeared again, she had learned
to love the pale groove circling her slim finger.

Dublin Masque

My mother's royal accent made me blush;
it throbbed neon like my swollen heart
when we walked together to the shops.
I wanted her to shove her curly hair
inside a scarf, or wrap it round
a bunch of wire curlers.
I wanted her to wear a dull tweed coat,
wag a yellow Rothman's at any face
that turned to wonder at her coiffed syllables.
Why couldn't she just moan about the weather?

But she was a peacock, a full fan of color
spread across our grey estate. She was a light
that dazzled everyone but those who skulked
inside her long shadow. How could a child hide
a lady, or behind a puff of smoke?

Elegance

After a long autumnal raspberry tramp,
I'd lash home at teatime, arms prickling and raw
with bramble thorn, and ask "Mum, what's cooking?
I'm ravishing." For years, she'd just smile,
stretch her long neck, and say, "I'm glad someone
thinks so," and point to the stacked bread bin
behind the nail polish.

And later, a teen reeling in the back door,
pink with cold, arms full of haw and heather,
Mother would chide, "Get that muck off your face.
You look like the wreck of the Hesperus."
I knew she meant some ship's vestige,
dried-up bark on some foreign shore.
But as I peeled off my wellies, and
flanneled my face, I always thought
of that early star rising, a faint wink
of hope in a grey patch of sky:
how it held its own brief beauty
before splintering into the million
others pebbling the black night.

How it wounded both of us to learn my name
meant *grace*. Mother, massaging glue along
the split ivory tusk her father brought
back from Africa, with her long, delicate
fingers, would whisper, *what did I know?*
and speak of heirlooms.

Leavetaking

Father, coffin-lid stiff on the staircase
extends a leaden hand across the banister

my brother, kid-bigger, hauls braced
bags out to the car, all perforated
tongue

while mother pries bran buns hot
from the oven to seal
in cellophane for the long
night drive to Shannon

hailstones thrash against the rusting
drainpipe, and choke into the gutter
sighing, *Time, there still is time.*

The Man at Immigration

says, "Don't think it is a right to come here."
Says, "It is a privilege." Luck eases back
into my throat like sediment. The man shuffles
papers, deals them like a deck of cards across a bar.
Says, "This country's drowning under foreigners."
He jolts the frets of my purse strings taut
before he studs each sheet with ink.

He seals what will become my own heart's warren.

I would have tossed the emerald in my pack
into his lap then. I would have thrust
my mother's fluted bijou into his hairy hands.
But a voice announced, "Keep each beast moving."
I plucked my stamped black book from the hatch,
and fled into the new night, singing.

Cross an ocean once, it's impossible to stop swimming.

Having Spoken Only Once

I knew you were the one
when I actually paused to consider
the cut of the wedding dress
on the vintage rack
and a tingle thrilled down my side,

when I could read Baudelaire
by candlelight, in the original,
gargle each glorious word, perfect
syllables for your sensitive ears.

I knew it was you when Escher
no longer drove me to drink
or to tears, when I had us sprawled
on my quilt in the Sunday sun,
melon peel and coffee mug rings
on the rug, the book review spread
on the floor, crossword done.

I was sure when I dredged up
the Volkswagen truck
and filled it with damson and corn
and two freckled baseball-capped kids,
a sheepdog in rear, and Bartok's
Hungarian Duos unfettered on the air

and years down the road,
you explaining the subtleties of Escher's
linear plot, as I stroke your thinning
hair, smooth your ingrained frown.

I could have sworn it was you
at the library who slid from the aisle

into Librarian's *Pick of the Week*:
a deft move, rapid, sleek.

Then I recognized me when I reached
to stroke the yellowing lace:
even bruised in a bunch
like this, it looked sweet,
but it felt stiff
and unfamiliar as your face.

Why I Cannot Marry the Art Critic

I try to tell my cousin
of my fear, that later, maybe not
for years, he may look elsewhere
for beauty, for satisfying.
She listens, silent.

I see her in her room, smoke
seething through her pulsing fingers,
receiver crooked under her chin.
A lone hand threads the cord
through gritted teeth, her lover
having left a moment before the sun
paled on their horizon, driving home
to cup his wife's uplifted,
eastward-turning cheek.

Lament for the Wanderer

Oh, oh sad-hearted Odysseus,
hair waving down your broad shoulders,
head drooping softly forward, a sea-embrace
lost on a shifting tide, your bow a knife
that Poseidon mocks, you aren't in your element,
are you, for all your fine loving and bellyful
of sweetmeats and wine, for all your booty and courage,
nor even the flaxen-haired women enchanting your feet
with bamboo; you'd give it all up in the flash of a god's
changing mood, wouldn't you, heroic Odysseus, wouldn't you,
for a chance to lose yourself in that woman's arms, she
of like-mind and heart, she who could reshape arithmetic
forging a glistening one of your two, in whose soft bed
aloneness is beautiful? She, half-woman, half-mad now,
who pines for you.

Don't you know, Fair Heart, that Circe would jewel a chalice
for your griefs, that Calypso's harp would string a concerto
of stars for one smile? Unguents threading through air,
if you would just look. Lift your face skyward, just try,
it might be up there you will find Penelope's gaze,
taunting the gods with her singular eyes.

Waitress at the Irish Pub

Okay, so it's my first day:
I don't know where to find
the HP sauce or vinegars,
and I slice the soda bread
way too thick. So, I can't
flip the napkins into scalloped
shells you might find washed up
on an Irish beach. It may take
time to remember whether *Limerick*
is ham or cheese, and whether *Yeats'*
Inisfree has fish strips or chutney.

But I do know where Limerick sits
— bleak, grey, soulless town —
and I know that the poor bastard
who sits proudly down in a booth
in his *I Love Ireland* teeshirt
wanting to treat himself Irishstyle
and asks what Dublin Coddle is,
and which berries make up trifle
(no matter how simple he may be)
deserves more than an upturned nose
from the waitress of experience,
and a "watch-me-deal-with-this-freak"
wink at me. Am I to learn the etiquette
of waiting from this?

I know a village idiot is sensitive
as you or me. I also know where Tipperary
is. And as I wipe away his crumbs, I show
him on the wall map, whisper it's a longer
way from here than the menu'd have him believe.

Zen, and More

for S.

I woke to a soft humming in my ear
this morning. All was black. I thought at first
it was those wasps, in hordes about my feet,
the ones inside the holes I'd jammed my legs
in, in my dream, the ones that greedily
pulled me like a drumstick towards them
with the fury of their hum. The *auwmmmm*

mmmmm thumped into my temple, spread across my skin,
until my veins picked up the pulse, the din,
and belted out a steady bass from some base within.
I ached for stillness, for a force to pull
me up, to loan me air again. I longed for breath,
and found it, then, on my tongue — the thick, sweet
scent of my love, done with his meditation, curved
above me, his chant still echoing after him
through a chink of open door from the garden.

How He Came to Me and Left

I. The Angel at My Lintel

Deliberate. The hand at the end of absence.
White knuckled fists at my door. Night
skitters over dustbins in the alley.
I suck it in like wind. Whole moons
shiver in the sky.

A cool, cream finger here
and here. We lick each swollen
bruise of time, of miles.
We bleed into each other's grooves.

— Shrouds of iris teeming, Ah!
hawks winging down our skin —

He has taught me this:

the pilgrim track of clouds
the ridges of the heart

how yeast rises and rises and rises.

II. Airplane

My hands spill out into thin air.
His form is everywhere
but here — shapechanging fingers,
limbs, damp hair. Hoops

of bone find me here or there or
here.

Nowhere
comes near to home.

Thin reeds of cloud drift in.
The foot of my heart is dancing,
I cannot believe my skin.
I am a rod — sheet lightning — I am struck.
Spun silver in the root of my gut. I am outside
myself. Drive that flesh back
in, back to where it must feed,
hollow, grateful for one remnant
clove of skin.

Echo

Was it your hands after all that spoke my name,
your hands joined like a heart at the wrist
that you cupped my face in? Did I lace my lips
through your fingers like a prayer?

Can I say they were yours after all there,
after the parting of lips
and the joining? How could we know
the geography of tongues?

What will I take from this,
from the burning hole in your palm,
from the white fury of bone under knuckle?

I will set my eyes on the sieve,
scrape up the ashes from your fist
with my nails.

Tell me, will I find a loose wisp
there to put to my ear?
Will it be chanting a lyric
or a long oboe of grief
that only a ghost can hear?

Embroideries

In my dream
I always wear the *broderie
anglaise* christening smock.
What's different is her breath
redolent of mint sprigs
and her dress, raw silk,
pure ivory, a luscious
nest to bury into.
Belgian cobweb lace drapes
in scallops down her breast.
And he, a warm intoxicant,
nuzzles softly into the cleft.
We are a blessed trinity,
swaddled in crimson velvet.
Never does he stamp his boot,
"Cut the curlers from her hair,
we'll be late to church!"
Never does the Bishop whip
my sliding jockey cap off
my sweating forehead, groaning.
Never do I stash my sullied
cotton frock down a bush
and parade the parish
in satin underpants,
my ears singed with
secondhand, secondhand.

Heart Attack

My *father is not here*
My *father is not here*
I hover round the house
from room to darkened room
stroking china cups, a teapot,
ladle cream slops into the jug.
I wrap the tea towel tight
around his mug.

Mother, later from the hall, needs
to know what time it is in the kitchen.
I say it is the same time everywhere.
She does not smile but winds the clock,
comforted, "There!" she says.
"I cannot bear stopped clocks."

He was to meet at the dock today, launch
into his usual foray about long-departed daughters.
I can't remember Father ever being gone,
not even for a night, always a fixture,
a given, like clouds or dawn or the surefire
clatter of the milkman's cart before
first light.

Who will fill the hot water bottles?
Who will polish the shoes? Who will pull
down rosary beads from the shelf
at night, and spread them, heart-shaped
about a votive candle? Who else will find space
among the crockery to invite the spirits in?

The Stranger at the Station

His goatee a black angle
still as October, and cold.
The sky salmon entrails at dusk.
The tag on his case.
An envelope, *Return to Sender.*

I know this place.
Air sour as harvest wine.
At dawn, the train will pull out,
one low drawl. The platform a memory.
His eyes, bullets.

Take him away.
Draw down the blinds. Fast.
Hide him from the winnowing grasses.
Give me lime spilling along the horizon
any day. *Any day.*

Irish Aubade

Cloistered in dark waves of hay,
glutted with love, we cleave
to warmth and to sleep, but

before the first vines of light
twist in on the eaves,
I will creep from this bower
and dance down to Lissadell.

Before the ring ouzel knells a new day,
I will weave a creel of sally rods
for my love, and in it I shall lay
sprigs of foxglove and luss, and a laurel
of Canterbury and harebell sprays.

And a cran I will strand
with honied willow and caramel rush
and place acorn and cobnut wreaths
there for my love.

And I will strew them glorious
about his still feet
so he may remember me,
for gossamer dulls in sunlight,
and I must leave,
I must go grieving back to cairns.

If You Lose Your Way

There are signs:
the mark on a lover's
chest, a cough, the track
of striations on marble.
There is a scar on parchment
to remind you of all your privations,
a red lozenge minding your past.

But now you are here, and
you will be led delicately
along the path you have so long needed.

Look for the lamp at the hem
of your garden. If it burns amber,
don't turn away. Let greyness itself
be a seam, if it is dark.

You have trawled the seasons
with your heart, looking for answers.
Now it is time to be still.
Let your sorrowing trail in a long quire
behind you.

Tonight, hold up your palm.
Let it become the thing
it was intended.

Let wind, let stars, let rain come.
Feel them drip-dripping off the eaves
of each slender, willing finger tip.

About the Author

Annie Callan was born in Dublin, Ireland. She earned an
M.A. in poetry from Johns Hopkins University in 1988. She
works variously as a teacher, a freelance journalist and a
consulting editor, and serves as literary escort for Oregon Book
Tours. Her writing honors include the Academy of American
Poets Award and the 1994 William Stafford Fellowship, as
well as prizes from Writers Digest, Willamette Writers, The
Portland Review, and Lake Oswego Literary Arts. She is
currently a guest lecturer in the Oregon Council for the
Humanities *Chautauqua* program.